FUNN BUSINI DOWN BELOW

A disgraceful little book of South Pembrokeshire jokes

Collected by Brian John

Greencroft Books

Trefelin, Cilgwyn, Newport, Pembrokeshire
SA42 0QN

Printed in Wales

CONTENTS

The jokes in this little collection have been gathered from a wide variety of sources, spoken and written. I thank all those who have sent material to me over the last few years, and my wife Inger for proof-reading and joke testing. I also acknowledge among my written sources publications by Irvin Cobb, Bob Phillips, Des MacHale, Bennett Cerf, Ashley Halsey, John Aye, and others. Very few of the jokes are original, and I am happy for them to be reproduced in any shape or form, in keeping with the great tradition of joke collections.

Illustrations: from Victorian children's comics and illustrated journals

Typesetting and design: Brian John on Apple Mac LC475

Photography and printing: Gwasg Gomer, Llandysul

ISBN: 0 905559 75 4

Introduction

Pembrokeshire is a county of two halves. South Pembrokeshire, otherwise known as "the Englishry" or as Little England Beyond Wales, has a character all of its own. Originally an Anglo-Norman colony, it has been a geographical enclave for almost a thousand years, bounded to the north and east by Welsh-speaking communities and to the south and west by the sea. Under its feudal lords it was peopled by immigrants from Flanders, Somerset and Hereford as well as Normandy. The native Welsh were either expelled or absorbed into the new culture.

The invisible line that demarcates Little England on its landward flanks came into being in the Middle Ages as a military frontier, and in the sixteenth century it was still possible for squire George Owen to demarcate its course exactly in his famous "Description of Pembrokeshire". The Landsker, as it came to be known, was initially so distinct that the peoples on either side of it spoke different languages, used their own unique farming methods, followed different customs, and even organised their communities in different ways.

As time went by contacts between the Englishry and the Welshry increased and the two communities were drawn more closely together by shared economic and social circumstances; but since South Pembrokeshire has always been the "economic powerhouse" of the county it has tended to gain in strength while the Welshry has suffered from rural decline, an ageing population, and an inexorable erosion of "Welshness". That having been said, both parts hang on on doggedly to their own languages and traditions.

The South Pembrokeshire community became, after the Conquest, a racial melting-pot, and it is not surprising that we find in its traditions, its dialect, its folk tales and its humour an extraordinary richness and diversity. Since, in this little book, we are concerned with South Pembrokeshire jokes, we have to recognise similarities with jokes from many different cultures. The jokes are somewhat more cosmopolitan than those of Welsh-speaking North Pembrokeshire, but the humour is still gentle rather than harsh, subtle rather than crude, and affectionate rather than cruel. As one might expect from a county with no large urban communities and no large-scale industrialisation (at least until recent decades), the jokes in circulation are about country and small-town eccentrics rather than smart jet-setting yuppies.

In this collection of jokes we can recognise a few stereotypes. For a start, the townies of Haverfordwest, Pembroke Dock and Milford have plenty of jokes about the slow old farmers of the villages and countryside. Relatively isolated villages like Marloes, Llangwm and Martletwy are fair game, and their natives are often portrayed as -- shall we say -- a little slow on the uptake. But the townies don't escape entirely, and there are plenty of jokes about their silly urban preoccupations and values which are put about by the good folks who live "up in the mountains." Many of the jokes in this collection come, as one might expect, directly from Newport, or Fishguard, or Crymych.

The term "down below" is widely used in the Welshry to describe the lowland, southern territory of the Englishry. But the term is not simply used with reference to altitude! Indeed, anybody who lives among "the mountain men" (as I do) will appreciate that the "down belows" are generally thought of as inferiors, deficient in linguistic, social and political skills and unable to appreciate the subtler things of life. And who am I, in my present circumstances, to disagree?

Finally, before letting you loose among the jokes, I need to explain that Little England is a cultural jewel, as different from Welsh-speaking Wales as Devon is from Ceredigion. Some misguided people have tried, within the last year or so, to pretend that the Englishry never really existed, that the Landsker was a figment of the imagination, and that South Pembrokeshire people should get up and learn Welsh like all good Welshmen. I profoundly disagree, and think that this is political correctness gone mad. Those who live in this little corner of Wales, neither fully Welsh nor fully English, are the guardians of a cultural tradition that goes back almost a thousand years. They deserve respect; and in a funny sort of way this collection of scurrilous jokes is a serious tribute to their resilience and their strength of character.

Brian John   **Christmas 1997**

Chapter One

ROLLING IN THE AISLES

Divine Intervention

The rector of Carew Cheriton Church was very worried. The church's tall Norman tower was in a poor state of repair, and the Church Restoration Fund was desperately short of cash. One day a friend convinced a millionaire to travel down to look at the Church, with a view to making a contribution to the repair work.

The vicar took the man around the outside of the tower, pointing out the cracks and the defective pointing. Then he showed him the inside of the tower, drawing his attention to the rotting timbers and crumbling plaster. The millionaire seemed very reluctant to help, but then a jackdaw dislodged a small piece of masonry from the top of the tower, and it fell down and struck the millionaire on the head. "Good gracious me!" he exclaimed. "I see that you really do have problems!" And with that he took out his cheque book and wrote out a cheque for £5,000. So the rector shouted to Heaven: "Go on, Lord! Hit him again!"

Acts of Faith

Three vicars from South Pembrokeshire -- one from Tenby, one from Neyland, and one from Marloes -- were suffering from overwork. Unknown to each other, they each booked in for a short break at the Christian Retreat Centre at Ffald-y-brenin in the Gwaun Valley. They got on well, and decided one day to go for a little fishing trip in Newport.

They hired a rowing boat, and since it was high tide they rowed up into the estuary, threw out the anchor and got on with some peaceful fishing. After a while the vicar from Tenby needed to answer the call of nature, so he walked across the water to the shore, went behind a bush, and then walked across the water back to the boat again.

Ten minutes later the vicar from Neyland got his hook caught on the bank after a long cast, so he walked on the water to release it and walked back to the boat the same way.

Ten minutes later the vicar from Marloes saw an old friend on the bank and decided to pop ashore for a little chat. He jumped over the side of the boat and sank into the water up to his neck, with great gurgling and splashing. As the other two vicars hauled him out, the one said to the other: "Bother! I knew we should have told him where the stepping stones were!"

Additional Baggage

The new young minister at Tabernacle in Haverfordwest was very enthusiastic, and managed to make a good impression on the bulk of the congregation during his first sermon. Afterwards, outside the chapel entrance, there was animated discussion about the young man's merits. Miss Griffiths let everybody know that she was not impressed. He was too young to know the ways of the world; his sermon was too learned by far; his choice of hymns left a great deal to be desired; his voice was too soft; and in his prayers he totally forgot to ask the Lord's blessing on the starving children of China.

"I have to say, ladies," she concluded, "that I shall be going home to my dinner this morning feeling that I am not carrying anything at all away with me."

"Perhaps, Miss Griffiths," said old Davy Jenkins, who happened to overhear her, "tha didn't bring anythin' to put it in."

A Fine One to Talk

A Baptist minister of religion was travelling with the Green's Motors bus one Sunday lunch-time from Haverfordwest to Milford, having just conducted Sunday morning worship in the county town. When the bus stopped in Merlin's Bridge a young man got on and sat himself down in the seat next to the minister. The minister was appalled when he realised that the young man was drunk.

"Young man," he said quietly, "I am truly sorry to see you in such a condition, and on the Sabbath too! Alcohol is a frightful curse which causes much misery and leads good folks away from the straight and narrow. With all my heart I beg you to turn over a new leaf. Give up the demon drink and the Lord will bless you and protect you as you sail through the tempestuous waters of life."

The young man gave the minister a serious looking over, and replied: "What the devil's tha talkin' about, mister? Tha's a fine one to talk! Tha's so drunk thaself that tha don't even know which way round to fix thy collar!"

Accidents will Happen

A holidaymaker came into the pub on the main road in Johnston one wet autumn evening, looking very shocked. The locals sat him down and somebody got him a stiff drink. When he had recovered his composure, he asked in a shaky voice "Is there a large black dog in this village with a white collar?"

The locals consulted for while and at last the publican said: "We don't think so, mister. None of us can recollect any such animal as you describe."

"Oh dear!" moaned the visitor. "As I thought -- I've just run over the vicar!"

Not Too Bad Considering

The vicar of St Mary's Parish Church in Pembroke was leaving for greener pastures, and he was visiting as many of his parishioners as possible to say his fond farewells. He met old Lenny Beynon in the park, and the old man shook his hand warmly.

"No doubt about it, boy. I'll be sad to see thee go, for the next one won't be half as good as thee."

The vicar was flattered at this compliment, and said: "No, no. I'm sure the next vicar will be an excellent man, quite as able to look after the parish as I have been."

"Why no boy," continued Lenny. "I knows what I'm talkin' about. Been here under five vicars, I has, and each new one have bin worse than the last."

No Escaping Politics

There was a christening service going on in the Methodist Chapel in Tenby. The service was under way when an elderly couple arrived, checking their watches and obviously in a bit of a panic. A sidesman met them at the church porch and said "Good morning to you! Are you with the Christening Party?" "Good Lord no!" replied the gentleman. "Been a Liberal all my life, and proud of it!"

A Private Affair

Miss Hallelujah Harries was giving a Religious Instruction lesson to Class 4D of the Secondary Modern School in Haverfordwest. She was expounding on the Creation. It was tough going, and she was finding it difficult to hold the attention of the class. Suddenly Sammy Williams, the least attentive of all her pupils, stuck up an arm and shouted: "Please miss, can I say something?"

"Yes Sammy, you may," replied Miss Harries. "Now then, what beautiful thought would you like to share with us?"

"Please miss, my dad says that we are descended from the apes."

"That may be so, Sammy," said the teacher. "But your private family matters are really of no concern to the rest of the class."

A New Face

The Thomas family were newly arrived in Haverfordwest, and started to attend St Martin's Church. Every Sunday morning Mr and Mrs Thomas would attend the family service with their little son Tommy, and in due course the lad became quite familiar with the vicar's face.

One Sunday morning another minister was filling the pulpit, and Tommy appeared rather troubled. At last he could contain himself no longer. He leaned over to his mother and said in a very audible whisper: "Mam, I wonder what's happened to St Martin?"

Just in Time

Brother Albert was a novice who had joined the monastic community of Caldey a couple of years previously. His reasons for giving his life to God were complicated, but included a failed and tempestuous love affair with a very beautiful young lady called Mary. One day he was greatly surprised when his ex-fiancee turned up on the island and asked if they could have a quiet talk in the monastery guest house.

Albert took the advice of the Abbott, who said he should go ahead and confront his past. So with some trepidation Brother Albert walked down to the guest house, and there met Mary. She looked more beautiful than ever, and it did not take very long before the conversation faded, to be replaced by a passionate embrace. Suddenly there was a knock on the door.

"Oh, Mary!" exclaimed Brother Albert. "That must be the Holy Ghost. Just in the nick of time."

Holy Teamwork

A holidaymaker who was staying near Haverfordwest decided that he would go along to the Sunday morning service in the little Methodist Chapel at Portfield Gate. After the service he chatted for a while with the old gentleman who had taken the collection.

"Very nice service indeed," he said. "The prayers and the singing were marvellous. Most uplifting. But the sermon went on a bit, and it was most upsetting that the learned discourse was interrupted every now and then by the organist with her coughing."

"Oh don't you worry about that," said the old man. "That's holy teamwork for you. Maisie coughs once when five minutes is gone, twice when ten minutes is gone, and three times after a quarter of an hour. Today the pastor got a bit carried away, an' forgot the signals. The terrible fit of coughin' that Maisie had after twenty minutes meant that her roast beef was burnin' in the oven, an' that if the last hymn didn't come quick she'd be off to rescue the Sunday dinner!"

No Recollection

Billy Bitter was propping up the lamp-post in the main street in Narberth when he was approached by the local Baptist minister.

"I am so glad to see that the Lord has shown you the error of your ways, and that you have turned from the darkness into the light," said the minister.

"Who, me?" asked Billy, extremely puzzled.

"Why yes, it was such a great pleasure to have you with us at our prayer meeting last night, celebrating the love of Jesus and asking forgiveness for our sins."

"Well, I'll be buggered," said Billy, slowly remembering. "So that's where I went to get out o' the rain!"

The Red-haired Reverend

Once upon a time the Methodist Chapel in Carew had a red-haired minister, whom we shall call Elijah Jenkins. Actually he was bald as a billiard ball, but his wig was very famous in the community, and on Sundays when he was in the pulpit with his eyes closed in prayer small boys in the chapel balcony would try to dislodge it with long sticks. Sometimes, to the great delight of the congregation, they succeeded.

According to legend, when Elijah got married he kept his secret from his new wife. On their wedding night, in spite of hectic activity in the marital bed, the wig stayed in position, and the happy couple subsided into a deep sleep.

In the middle of the night Elijah woke up briefly, took off his wig, and went back to sleep. Shortly afterwards his wife, half awake, began to feel amorous again, and stretched out her hand to caress the head of her beloved. She encountered a smooth bald head, and immediately said: "Now then, reverend, I knows tha likes to get up to a few tricks in bed, but for God's sake get thy bum off the pillow!"

Lesson for the Day

A famous evangelist was visiting Haverfordwest, where he preached every evening in the Temperance Hall on the evils of drink. One of his little tricks was to produce a bottle of whisky, a tumbler, and a wriggling worm, which he would place on the table in front of him. On this particular evening he went through his routine by pouring some whisky into the tumbler and then placing the worm in the whisky. The audience looked on, with mouths agape, as the worm expired before their very eyes.

""Now then, dearly beloved brothers and sisters," roared the evangelist, "what does that teach us about the demon drink?"

And Bobby Mathias shouted from the back row: "If you've got worms, for God's sake pour yourself a good glass of whisky!"

Tried to the Limit

Billy and Bertie Griffiths were two old bachelor brothers who were stalwarts of the little Methodist Chapel at Portfield Gate. They occupied adjacent bedrooms in the old family home, and contrived to keep body and soul together by selling eggs and produce from their smallholding.

Unfortunately their prize cockerel took sick, and Billy agreed to stay up late at night as he tried to nurse it back to health. About midnight he rushed in from the chicken shed and shouted up the stairs: "Bertie! Bertie! The cockerel have died."

There was no reply, and Billy shouted the same message up the stairs over and over again, still without any response.

At last Bertie could not stand the noise any longer. "Go to hell!" he shouted. "Damn and blast, can't tha see that I'm sayin' me prayers for that bloody cockerel?"

A Beautiful Epitaph

There was a new assistant at Havard the Monumental Masons in Haverfordwest. He had never taken an order for a grave headstone before, and when the recently-bereaved Gertie Beynon rang up to make arrangements for her husband's grave the conversation became somewhat confusing.

Gertie kept on giving detailed instructions as to the dimensions and precise placing of the lettering. After a while the assistant confirmed that he had understood everything, and advised Mrs Beynon that the marble headstone would be in place in three weeks' time.

In due course Mrs Beynon received the bill for the work, and went along to Prendergast Cemetery with a bunch of flowers in her hand to inspect the headstone. There it was, nicely cemented in, with the following inscription in beautiful gold lettering:

"To the memory of Billy Beynon, died 23rd March 1923 aged 63, nice and big, beloved husband of Gertie Beynon, a bit smaller. Rest in peace not too high and not too low, and if there is room we shall meet in Heaven."

Burying the Hatchet

In the bad old days there was great animosity between the Methodists and the Baptists in Pembroke Dock. As the years passed nobody could remember the original cause of the trouble, but it continued nonetheless. At last, a new young Baptist minister arrived, and decided that he would start to mend some bridges. So he went to visit the Methodist minister, and said: " It is high time that we put these old problems behind us, my brother. After all, we are both doing the Lord's work, are we not?"

"Indeed we are, brother," said the Methodist minister. "I quite agree that we must move forward together in the name of the Lord. We must work for the Lord to the best of our ability, you in your small way and I in His."

More Pressing Problems

"And it is written in the Good Book of Revelation" roared the evangelist, "that the world will come to an end on 1st January in the year 2000 AD, and all those who do not repent will rot in hellfire and damnation!"

"A load of old clap-trap," shouted Georgie Griffiths from the back row. "The world will go on and on, an' I'll bet thee half a crown that we will all still be here on 2nd January 2000 AD. You can pay me the day after."

"Aha! I see we have a doubter in our midst," said the evangelist, not used to being disturbed in the middle of the fire and brimstone. "Let me tell you, brother, that when the world really does come to an end as written in the scriptures, you will look pretty stupid, let me tell you."

"Indeed yes," shouted Georgie, beginning to enjoy himself. "If the world does come to an end like you says and when you says, I will surely look pretty stupid. But let me tell you, brother, that will be the least of me problems!"

Utterly Divine

In the days of Women's Lib, when lots of highly motivated ladies were going around making statements about one thing and another, a most attractive girl turned up at the door of St David's Cathedral in a topless dress, intent upon attending Matins. The Rural Dean, who happened to be close at hand, took her to one side and said: "I'm very sorry, Madam, but I can't allow you into the Cathedral dressed like that."

"I am making a statement," replied the girl, "and in any case I have a divine right." "I quite agree," said the Dean, "and you have a divine left too, but I still can't let you in."

All in Good Time

A young minister was just starting in Zion Chapel in Begelly, and before his first service he asked the advice of the steward, Reuben Walters. "Tell me now truthfully, Reuben," said the young man, "how long do you like your sermons to be in this chapel?"

"No hard an' fast rules," replied Reuben. "But if I was thee, boy, jest keep thy eyes open. When they looks at their watches don't tha worry -- a bit of sufferin' don't do them no harm. But when the watches is bein' listened to an' shook about, then if I was thee I'd get on quick to the last hymn!"

Small Mercies

The Rev Jeremiah Jones was evangelizing down in Angle, and since there was not much other entertainment in the village his gospel tent was was packed out every evening for his services. The locals were however reluctant to part with any coins when the hat went round for the collection, and on the last evening of the crusade Jeremiah blessed the few copper coins with the words: "We thank thee, Lord, for these bountiful offerings for the spreading of thy Gospel, and we also thank thee that I got my hat back."

Chapter Two

LARGER THAN LIFE

A Symbolic Gesture

According to legend, Major Gwilym Lloyd George, who was the MP for Pembrokeshire for many years after his first election in 1922, was proving to be a bit of a liability to the Tory Party. The Prime Minister, Harold MacMillan, thought it would be a good idea to put him out of harm's way in the House of Lords. So one day in 1957 MacMillan suggested to him that he might like to make the move from the Commons. Gwilym was not too keen on the idea since over the years he had got used to the House of Commons, but he promised that he would think about it.

Some time later MacMillan approached him again and put further pressure on him, and after due deliberation Gwilym said "All right, Prime Minister, I will make the move if you think it is in the best interests of the party."

"Splendid, splendid!" said the Prime Minister. "What would you like to take as your title? Choose something appropriate from your home area."

"As you know, I am very fond of Pembrokeshire," replied Gwilym. "Would it be acceptable if I give some thought to choosing a name from the very lovely area around Saundersfoot and Tenby?" The Prime Minister was delighted, and Gwilym went away to give the matter further thought.

Next time the two men met in the corridors of power Gwilym said "Prime Minister, I have made up my mind which name to use in my title."

"Splendid, splendid," said MacMillan. "Tell me what it is, and I will set the wheels in motion."

"I have decided," said Gwilym, "on a beautiful title. In future, I wish to be known as --- Lord Stepaside."

Sadly, the Prime Minister would not accept the title, and Gwilym ended up being called plain Viscount Tenby.

A Strange Mystery

Larry Legless and Sam Stout were well known in the county town for drinking more than was good for them. One evening, as they sat slumped in the corner of the Bumbles and Flies down by the Old Bridge, the following conversation was heard to pass between them. "Good evenin' sir!" said Larry. "Now then, have I not seen thee afore somewhere?"

"Wouldn't be surprised," replied Sam, "since I've been about a tidy bit over the years. Maybe we met up some time down in Tenby?"

"Couldn't have bin me. Never bin to Tenby in me life."

"Not me neither. But there's a funny thing for thee. The question is, who the hell was them two chaps that met up in Tenby?"

Order of Priorities

One of the great characters of the Pembrokeshire agricultural scene was Douglas Morris of Burton. He was one of the pioneers of local turkey breeding, and he built up a successful business which he ran from his farm. He sold many thousands of fresh turkeys to local butchers shops, but in the early days he also sold directly by advertising in the local press. One year, long before the advent of the ansafone, he placed the following advert in the West Wales Guardian: "Top quality fresh turkeys for sale for your Christmas table. Buy local for best value. Phone your order now, but not during the News or Tom and Jerry."

Enough to Get On With

One day a delegation called on Freddie Jenkins at his home in Tenby and asked him if he would like to stand in the County Council elections. He was very reluctant, but the members of the delegation pressed him hard, making points about duty and responsibility, and the need for a good Tory to represent the local area as an independent candidate. However, Freddie was adamant that he had neither the time nor the inclination to become a county councillor. He concluded the interview by saying: "Gentlemen, I thanks thee from the bottom of me heart for the great honour of askin' me to stand agin the sittin' councillor Tommy Nicholas in this 'ere election. But I has to say, with great reluctance, that I ain't in no position just now to neither stand in the vote nor sit on the council, since I finds meself constantly on the run. I has a wife, a teenage daughter, a mortgage, a third-hand car, and two bloody poodles, an' I reckons that is quite enough trouble for one man."

Honours Galore

After an illustrious career Col Albert Jones of Haverfordwest retired from the army, having been showered with honours. Shortly after arriving home he was invited to the Shire Hall to review a parade of Territorial Army recruits. He turned up in his old uniform, with his breast covered with medals, and during the parade he impressed the recruits no end with his military bearing and immaculate appearance.

Afterwards, over a cup of tea in the officer's mess, he was asked by the TA sergeant about his decorations. "Where on earth did you get all those medals, colonel?" he asked. "Was it for some heroic deed, or did you lead your men to victory in some great battle in the War?"

"Why no, boy," replied Albert. "Nothin' so complicated. This one by here is the Victoria Cross. A's the first one I got, an' I got'n by mistake in the First World War. Then I got all the other ones because I got that one."

A Nice Lie In

Dicky and Nellie were a happily married old couple from Carew, who were somewhat confused during the Second World War while the air raids were going on over the area. Instructions came down from on high that all houses had to fit blinds or curtains so as to achieve a total blackout, and a neighbour called Jeb kindly helped the old couple to complete the job.

Three days later Jeb and the other neighbours became seriously worried since they had not seen the old couple since the blackout was installed. They hammered furiously on the front door, and eventually a bleary-eyed Dicky came to the door in his pyjamas. "That's a relief to see you, Dicky," said Jeb. "We thought you was both dead!"

"Why no, boy," replied Dicky. "In bed we are, waitin' for it to get light!"

Most Efficacious Treatment

Vince Griffiths from Carew was suffering something terrible from the constipation. So he went to see Doctor Proctor, who prescribed a bottle of strange liquid and instructed him to take three teaspoons a day until things got moving again.

Three days later the good doctor happened to meet Vince in the street. "Good day, Mr Griffiths!" he said. "Are you feeling better?"

"Yes indeed, doctor," replied Vince. "Much improved."

"And have you managed to pass anything today?"

"Why aye, boy," said Vince. "Two dogs an' a horse and cart, when I was comin' up past the chapel."

Chapter Three

PEOPLE IN TOWNS

Nice and Friendly

Councillor Byron Hill of Pembroke Dock was used to getting his way, and reckoned that he knew everybody in town well enough to go through life without too much hassle. He frequently parked on double yellow lines and got away with it on the basis that he was "on council business", but one day a new traffic warden came riding into town.

Eagle-eyed and keen as mustard, the new man spotted Councillor Hill's car parked in an illegal place while the great man was showing a visitor around the empty shops. He took out his little book and was in the process of writing out a parking ticket when the Councillor and his guest returned. "Just you watch me," whispered the Councillor to his guest. "Nobody pushes me around in this here town."

The Councillor took a five-pound note out of his wallet and handed it to the traffic warden while he said: "Now then, young man, you probably don't know me, but I'm Councillor Byron Hill and I'm here on official council business." The traffic warden handed the five-pound note back again and said: "Well, isn't that nice, sir, because I'm Billy Jenkins and so am I."

"Now look here," protested the Councillor, getting red in the face, grinding his teeth and clenching his fists. "Surely we can handle this in a friendly way?"

"Certainly sir," said the traffic warden, calm as anything. "I'll smile when I give you this parking ticket, and you can smile when you take it from me."

The Trials of the Artist

Constable Constable was a part-time policeman in Honey Harfat who fancied himself as a bit of an artist. Every weekend, and on his days off, he set out into the wilderness with his painting kit and slaved away at his masterpieces. He once exhibited a painting of a lump of rock in the Camrose village hall, but if the truth were told he was not really a very good artist. However, undaunted, he considered himself to be greatly talented and spent much time criticising the works of art produced by other local artists. He considered that they were mere dabblers with no understanding of the essence of real art; and he frequently held court in the Mariners Hotel bar on the mysteries of real art.

One day he walked into the bar and collapsed into a chair, pronouncing himself to be quite exhausted both mentally and physically from his efforts out on Strumble Head. "You would never believe it," he said to the barmaid, "but I've been trying to paint the lighthouse for three whole days, and I still haven't managed to get the subtleties of colouring just right."

"What a pity," said the barmaid sweetly. "Have you tried using one of those new rollers with a long, long handle?"

Not Entirely Useless

A small boy walked into Billy Clog's cobblers shop in Manorbier, carrying a very ancient pair of boots in his hands. "Please sir," said the small boy, "Mother says please to mend these boots and how much will it cost."

Billy examined the old boots carefully and gave his prognosis. "Well, young man," he said, "you go home an' tell your Mam that if I fits a new pair of uppers, an' then replaces the heels an' soles on them, they will be as good as new. Twelve an' sixpence that will be. You can tell her there's nothin' much wrong with the laces."

Not Much Chance

A young man called in at a well-known kennels in Pembroke and asked the proprietor whether he had any white dogs. "We have all sorts of white dogs," said the proprietor. "Which breed would you be wantin' ?"

"Well," replied the young man with a perplexed look on his face. "I'm not rightly sure. I knows what it looks like, but not the name. It is about two foot tall, like a sort of greyhound but with shorter legs, and like a sort of bulldog but with a longer nose. Then it has a droopy tail and ears that sticks up a bit. The coat is sort of shiny an' a bit more curly than a sheepdog's coat. An' it runs like the wind an' sort of yaps instead of barkin'. Do you by any chance keep any such dogs?"

"No I do not," replied the dealer emphatically. "Very seldom it is that I gets any dogs like the one you are describin', but when I gets 'em I drowns 'em."

Nice and Peaceful

Tommy Philpin from Llangwm had to go up to Cardiff on business, but it was a very busy week and he could not find a cheap B&B anywhere. At last he found a place, but the landlady said "I have only one bed left in the house, but I have to warn you that it's in a room with another gentleman who snores horribly. You probably won't sleep a wink."

"I'll take it," said Tommy, and so he moved his bag up to the room and settled in. Next morning, when Tommy came down to breakfast, the landlady asked him whether he had managed to get any sleep. "Why aye, girl," said Tommy. "No bother at all. Afore I turned the light out I went over to his bed an' gave'n a big kiss. After that, a stayed awake all night while I slept like a baby."

To be Frank

There was once a famous artist in Harfat who made a speciality of life drawings. One morning he was at work in his studio when there was a knock on the door. A large lady came in, and without looking up he said "Madam, take your clothes off behind the screen and then go and relax on that sofa." The woman did as she was told, and reclined on the sofa in the nude. Then just as the artist was about to start sketching, she said: "Doctor, I want you to be quite frank and tell me just what is wrong with me."

Taken aback, the artist looked at her closely and then said: "Well, madam, I have three things to tell you. First, you are about three stones overweight. Second, your beauty would be much improved if you stopped using all that horrible makeup. And third, I am Horatio Evans the artist, waiting for my new model to arrive. Doctor Erasmus Jones lives on the next floor up."

Not Actually Needed

Gerald James had a little general store in Haverfordwest before the First World War. One Friday in the year 1910 he was behind his counter when a very scruffy little boy came in, looking somewhat ill at ease. Gerald had never seen him before. "What can I do for you, young man?" he asked. "Please sir, my mam says please to sell me a roll of toilet paper."

Gerald took down a roll from the shelf and said "That will be threepence, please." The boy paid over the money, took the toilet roll and scuttled out of the shop.

First thing on Monday morning the little boy was back again, carrying the toilet roll under his arm and carrying a letter in his hand. "Please sir," he explained, "my mam says please to read the letter." Gerald opened it up and read as follows:

"Dear Sir, Billy is taking the roll of toilet paper back to you, and please to pay him the money back what he paid you. We will not be needing the toilet roll. Our visitors never came."

No Comparison

Once upon a time there was a prosperous businessman in High Street, Haverfordwest, by the name of Billy White. His business was a thriving one, but when he died it was taken over by a Chinaman named Mr Wong. He had little idea of how to run a business, and things started to decline, and then went from bad to worse. At last his brother came down from London in order to help out -- but it was to no avail, and the business was eventually declared bankrupt. Afterwards the sad episode was said by many people in Haverfordwest to prove quite conclusively that two Wongs can never make a White.

A Job Well Done

Dai the Tooth. the Harfat dentist, had just completed a major job on a patient, who had had to suffer the agonies of six major fillings at one sitting. "There now, Mr Jenkins," said Dai. "Six large holes all filled successfully. They shouldn't give you any more trouble."

"Water! Water!" gasped the patient, looking pale and distinctly the worse for wear. "I must have a glass of water!"

The dentist's assistant handed him a glass of pink water. He took a big mouthful and swilled it around his teeth for a long time. Then he patted his cheeks and throat with the towel, and finally spat the water out with a great sigh of relief.

"All right now?" asked Dai. "Were you feeling faint?"

"Oh no," replied the patient. "I was just checkin', after havin' all them holes drilled, that me mouth will still hold water."

A Simple Mistake

Yamaha Jenkins enjoyed roaring up and down the streets of Milford on his extremely large motor bike. One day his friend Bert prevailed upon him to take him for a high speed run. Yamaha agreed, but he said to Bert: "You haven't got the proper leathers, pal, and at 100 mph it gets a bit chilly on the back of a big bike. If I was you I'd put your overcoat on back to front so as to keep out the wind." Bert did as he was told, and off they roared.

Half-way down Charles Street the bike went over one of those horrible traffic calming bumps at high speed. Bert went flying off the passenger seat and landed in a crumpled heap in the middle of the road. Yamaha was horrified, and after turning his bike round he returned to the scene of the accident.

He pushed his way through the crowd of locals who had gathered around in order to help the casualty. "Is Bert all right?" he asked.

"Well," said a helpful gentleman, "he was until we turned his head round the right way."

That's More Like It

A smartly-dressed customer walked into Griffiths Grocer in Narberth one day and explained that he was looking for some exotic cheeses for a very important dinner-party. He insisted that the cheeses were to be "fairly lively", but after being shown some Brie, some Gorgonzola and some Danish Blue, he was not satisfied. He could not even be encouraged to approve of an extremely ripe Danish Havarti. At last, having exhausted all the possibilities, Mr Griffiths was moved to sarcasm. He turned to his assistant and said "Now then Jimmy, you'll have to go out in the yard. Take that No 9 mature Cheddar off the chain and bring it in, but watch out that the bugger don't bite you."

Chapter Four

FARMERS AND PEASANTS

No Real Value

An old farmer from Camrose was going about his business when he noticed that some holidaymakers had stopped their car in the lane near his orchard. The family of four had all climbed over the hedge, and there they were, collecting up fallen fruit from the grass beneath the heavily-laden trees.

Some time later the holidaymakers returned to their vehicle, to find the farmer leaning against the hedge chewing on a piece of straw. "Oh hello," said the father. "We helped ourselves to some of the fallen fruit in your orchard, which was only going to go rotten if it was left there any longer. We hope you don't mind."

"Oh, that's all right," replied the farmer. "While you was away I helped meself to some o' the tools from the back o' your car, which looked as if they was gettin' a bit rusty an' needed a good home."

The Annual Migration

The American visitor was talking to Farmer Watkins from Spittal, and the conversation got onto the weather. "Say," said the American, "how is it here in the winter? Get a lot of snow and ice?"

"Oh, terrible! terrible!" replied the farmer. "Last year we had snow-drifts up to the top of the kitchen door. And the gales is something horrendous -- the north wind never stops from December to April. A hundred miles an hour is nothin' unusual. And the rain! You would never believe it if you was to see it, my friend. By damn, it's a miracle we manages to survive."

"It sounds worse than Alaska," said the American, suitably impressed. "So how do you manage to pull through till the warm spring weather arrives?"

"Oh, I goes south to the sun with the missus for a few weeks every winter," said the farmer, "in order to stave off the melancholia."

"Very sensible indeed. To Tenerife maybe? Or perhaps Madeira?"

"Why no boy. Amroth."

A Nice Little Deal

A sociology professor from Oxford University was staying in Marloes while he researched into the ways of quaint country folk. One evening he went into the village pub for a quiet pint, and got talking to a local farmhand called Davy Dawdle. "Very fond of riddles we are, around here," said Davy.

"Is that so?" said the professor. "How very interesting. Tell you what, why don't you try some on me?" "Oh all right," replied Davy. "And tha can try some on me too."

Then the professor said: "Just to make it more interesting, I'll pay you a pound every time I miss a riddle, and you pay me a pound every time you miss one." "But that ain't fair," said Davy. "Tha'art an educated man an' I don't know nothin'. It'll be fairer if I pays thee fifty pence an' tha pays me a quid."

The professor agreed, and after thinking for a while Davy came up with this riddle: "What has three legs walking, four legs swimming and one leg flying?"

The professor couldn't work it out, and at last said: "I have to admit I don't know the answer. Here's a pound."

"Well there's a funny thing," said Davy. "I don't know the answer neither. Here's fifty pence change."

A Helping Hand

Eddie Egghead was a bit slow, but he worked hard, and between them he and his dad managed to get a reasonable living off their little farm near Marloes.

One day he stuck his head round his neighbour's kitchen door and said: "Mornin' John. Ca'st tha help me to right a load of manure that I has accidentally tipped over down by the gate of thy big meadow?"

"Right enough, Eddie," replied John. "But I'm jest sittin' down for me dinner. Come on in an' join me for a bite to eat."

"I ain't sure Dad would like that," said Eddie -- but the food smelt good and he allowed himself to be persuaded.

An hour later, the neighbour said: "Now then, better jest listen to the cricket on the wireless afore we tackles that there truck down by the gate. Things is gettin' interestin' down at Trent Bridge." "I ain't at all sure that Dad would like that," said Eddie, but then he forgot all about it and listened to the cricket.

About three hours after the accident John got up, yawned, and said to young Eddie: "Now then lad, we'd better go an' sort out thy pile o' manure. Why don't we call thy Dad to come an' give us a hand?"

"Oh, didn't I tell thee?" said Eddie. "A's under the manure."

Unsound Advice

A holidaymaker was driving along a country road one warm summer afternoon near Wiseman's Bridge when his engine stalled. He lifted the bonnet and pottered about for a while with the electrical connections. Still the car would not start. At last, frustrated and angry, the motorist sat down in the hedge and waited for another motorist to come along who might be able to give him some help.

A few minutes later a herd of cows came down the road, heading towards a nearby farm for the evening milking. Several of the cows ambled past, and then the motorist was greatly surprised when one of them looked under the raised bonnet of the car and said "From what I can see, your problem is probably a blocked carburettor."

The man was greatly surprised at this. At last, when all the cows had gone past, the farmer came along with a long stick in his hand and his sheepdog at his heel. "I say," said the man. "One of your cows just looked under the bonnet of my car and said I had a blocked carburettor!"

"Was it a big white one with a speckled face and a black rump?" asked the farmer.

"Yes Yes, that was the one," said the holidaymaker.

"That would be Buttercup then," replied the farmer. "If I was you, I wouldn't listen to her. She don't know nothin' about cars."

Accurate as Ever

The Pembrokeshire County Show has for many years been the premier agricultural event on the calendar, and attendance figures have been rising every year. However, at the annual meeting of the Show organizers in 1966 some complaints were made that the official attendance figures were greatly exaggerated. The Show's president-elect Mr Wilfred Davies had to cope with a somewhat acrimonious discussion on the topic, but then he intervened and brought the discussion to a most satisfactory conclusion.

"Now then gentlemen," he said. "You know how it is. Somebody asks for the attendance figure. So one of us officials climbs up on the roof of the secretary's office, takes a look around, and says "Oh, that looks like 21,385". So that becomes the official figure, and that's that."

Detailed Directions

A holidaymaker from Hemel Hempstead was lost in the countryside not far from Marloes, but after driving around for a while without a map to help him, and with yelling kids in the back of the car, he spied two farmers leaning on a gate.

Excuse me please, gentlemen," he said. "I am trying to get to Walwyn's Castle. Can you help me by telling me the way?"

The two old timers conferred in loud whispers for a long time, and then one of them said: "Very sorry indeed, mister, but we ain't precisely sure. Neither of us has never been to Walwyn's Castle. So sad to say, we don't know the way."

"Oh dear. But thank you anyway," said the lost holidaymaker, and drove off up the road. Then he noticed in his rear mirror that the farmers were both waving after him furiously. He stopped the car and they ran up after him. "Would it help," panted one of them, "if we was to tell you the way to St Ishmael's?"

"It might," said the driver. "I think that may be somewhere near our destination."

"Well there's a pity," said the other farmer, "since we don't know the way to St Ishmael's neither."

Problem on the Mountain

Billy and Bert were farm workers from Cosheston way, and having saved up for two years, they set off on the holiday of a lifetime, to do some skiing in the Swiss Alps. They were both dyslexic, but thought that their little problem wouldn't matter too much in foreign parts.

All went well for the first few days of the week, when the two friends were confined to the nursery slopes with their ski instructor. Then he sent them and the rest of the group off up the ski lift to the mountain top to descend by themselves. Somehow Billy and Bert got separated from the others, and found themselves at the top of a steep descent. They tried to remember the advice of their instructor before launching themselves into the unknown. "Now then," said Billy, "a said that if we zig-zags down, we won't have no problem at all."

"No no," replied Bert. "I'm sure as eggs is eggs that a said we was to zag-zig down the slope. If we zig-zags instead we might get in a hell of a caffle."

So the friends stood on top of the mountain, debating whether they were to zig-zag or zag-zig down the piste. At last a man came along, dragging a sledge behind him. Bert waved at him and shouted "Excuse me, mister, but please can tha tell me an' me mate whether we are supposed to zig-zag or zag-zig down this bloody hill?"

"Sorry I can't help," replied the man. "I know nothing at all about skiing. I'm just a tobogganist."

"That's a pity," said Billy. "I suppose we'll just 'ave to wait for somebody with skis to show up. But tell thee what. We'll have a packet of Woodbine an' a box o' matches with thee while we are waitin'."

No Cause for Concern

Farmer Harries from Marloes was getting worried, since his hens had apparently stopped laying. For the last few mornings, when he went to collect the eggs he found the nesting boxes empty instead of containing the usual brown and shiny dozen. Next morning, just as it was getting light, he was awoken by a cackling noise from the poultry house. He dressed quickly and rushed down across the farm-yard to see what was going on. He opened the door of the shed and peered into the darkness. "Is there anybody there?" he called.

There was a long pause, and then a quavering voice replied: "Nobody at all, except for us chickens."

Cutting his Losses

Douglas Morris of Burton was a great character, and also one of Pembrokeshire's leading innovators in matters agricultural. One day he read that water buffaloes were going to be the meat producers of the future, so he bought a little calf. He fattened it up alongside a Hereford calf, but the latter put on much more weight than the water buffalo and started to bully it mercilessly. Douglas did not know quite what to do, but then he had a bright idea. In the next edition of "The Western Telegraph" the following advert appeared: "Wanted -- shorthand typist. Willing to exchange for one buffalo."

Reserving Judgement

An old fellow from Narberth was hauled up before the judge at the Assizes in Haverfordwest and charged with sheep stealing. Never having stolen a sheep before, he was not too familiar with the strange ways of the law.

"Guilty or not guilty?" thundered the judge.

"Hang on a bit, your Lordship," replied the prisoner. "How do thee expect me to know that, when I ain't even heard the evidence yet?"

Chapter Five

IN TIMES OF SORROW

Almost Time to Go

At the end of a funeral for one of the oldest residents of Honey Harfat, the undertaker noticed a very old man standing disconsolately outside the chapel. "How are you today, Mr Griffiths?" asked the undertaker.

"Not so good," replied the old man. "Time is catchin' up with me at last. Not many of us old fellers left, I'm afraid. And there goes poor old Dicky. We won't see his like again. Them that's left in town of our generation can be counted on one hand now. Bad business indeed."

"So how old are you, Mr Griffiths?"

"Ninety-three on my next birthday, but there's no knowin' if I'll see out the winter or even make it to the end of the week."

"Well then," said the undertaker, "if that's the case it's hardly worth you goin' home today, is it? Why don't you just settle down right here, nice and handy for the arrangements, and save us all a lot of bother?"

A Slight Delay

Marloes people were reputed, in the good old days, to be a bit slow on the uptake. According to legend, a gentleman was passing through the village one day when he encountered a funeral procession heading for the church. He took off his hat and stood with head bowed as the procession passed, and continued on his walk. Half an hour later he returned past the same spot, and was intrigued to see that all of the mourners were sitting on the grass outside the church gate, some of them enjoying a quiet smoke and some reminiscing about old times. The vicar was pacing up and down looking at his watch, and there was no sign of the hearse.

The gentleman approached the assembled company and asked what was going on. "Oh, nothing serious," replied an elderly mourner. "The hearse have gone back to Mullock Bridge. A'll be back in a couple o' minutes. Some silly bugger forgot the corpse."

Room for Doubt

There was a big funeral in Tabernacle Chapel in Milford, where the chief mourner was Bessie Williams. She had just lost her husband Tom, and there he was, up at the front of the chapel, screwed down in his coffin, as she sat there in the front pew accompanied by her daughter Dottie. Mourning she certainly was, but if the truth were told she had had a pretty tough time of it with old Tom's womanising, drinking and violence at home.

Because Tom had not been a chapel-going man the minister knew very little about him; but this did not deter him from launching into a most inspiring eulogy, in which he praised Tom's kindness, his love of family, his capacity for hard work, his thriftiness, and assorted other virtues. Bessie listened to all of this with increasing incredulity, and at last she nudged Dottie and whispered (quite loudly):

"By God, Dottie, I do believe we are at the wrong funeral. Pop up the front with thy screwdriver, just to check it ain't somebody else under that lid!"

Making Contact

Maisie Probert was grieving terribly after the loss of her beloved husband George until one of her neighbours told her that a famous medium was coming next day to Pembroke Town Hall to hold a seance. "Why don't you go along and see if you can make contact with George on the other side?" she said. "Once he reassures you that all is well, I am sure you'll be greatly relieved, and able to get on with normal life again."

Maisie agreed to go along to see the medium, and sure enough managed to make contact with her dear departed. "George! Is that really you?" she asked, full of excitement.

"Yes, Maisie, indeed it is", replied the voice of George from the ether.

"Are you all right? Are you being well looked after? And what do you do all day long?"

"Oh, I'm fine. Things get a bit boring at times, but the weather is always nice and warm, and every day I make love when I wake up, eat a bit, make love again, sleep a bit, make love again, eat a bit more, make love some more ...."

"Stop, stop!" cried Maisie. "Is that really what it's like in Heaven?"

"Oh, I'm not in Heaven," replied George. "I've become a Buddhist, and I'm a rabbit in Western Australia."

In Memoriam

There are lots of Johns in South Pembrokeshire, and it is reputed that somewhere this epitaph is to be seen on a headstone:

Here lies the bones of Jimmy Jones,
Who died from eating cherry stones.
His name was John it was not Jones
But Jones is put to rhyme with stones.

Chapter Six

EVERYDAY LIFE

No Great Hurry

The telephone rang in Dr Barton's surgery in Haverfordwest. When he answered, he discovered that there was an anxious gentleman on the other end. "Ah Doctor, I need your advice," he said. "Something has happened to my wife. She has this high temperature, and complains of a sore throat and acheing joints."

"Quite, quite," said the doctor. "That will be the flu bug that is doing the rounds. You will find that tomorrow she will lose her voice entirely."

"Is that so?" replied the gentleman, after a long pause. "Well, if you are up this way over the next six months, perhaps you could look in and see what you can do for her?"

Not in on the Secret

Between the Wars the temperance movement was in full swing in Haverfordwest, and there were frequent campaigns which concentrated on the evils of drink. One day a temperance speaker was on his soap box down on the Castle Square, developing a favourite theme. "It all starts with tobacco!" he shouted. "You think all you need is a quiet smoke! So you dash into the tobacconist round the corner and put down your money for a packet of Woodbines. But that, my friends, is not the end of it. You mark my words, for in the wake of those twenty cigarettes will follow beer, whisky, red wine, cider, rum and brandy!"

"My goodness, that sounds like a good offer," came a voice from the crowd. "Please to tell me the name of your tobacconist!"

Wrong Direction

In the bad old days of the Norman conquest, Gilbert de Clare, the lord of Haverford Castle, was awakened from his afternoon nap one day by a great commotion. The main gate of the castle was swung open, and a troop of his best soldiers came rushing in on horseback.

Their leader leapt off his horse and rushed up to the Lord's chamber. "Sire! Sire!" he shouted. "We have done your bidding, and have raped and pillaged the whole area round Jordanston!"

"You fool!" snapped Lord Gilbert. "I told you to rape and pillage around **Johnston**. We have no enemies around Jordanston."

"Sire, things have changed. I bring you hot news of new enemies!"

Quite a Different Matter

Billy Bumpkin of Marloes had a bit of a limp, and thought he'd better go in to the Surgery in Honey Harfat to get it sorted out. So next market day, after selling all his eggs, he popped up to see the doctor. "Funny business, doctor," said Billy. "I has this limp that is botherin' me a bit, and I thought I'd better check with thee in case it is on account of the fact that me right leg is a bit shorter than me left." So the doctor examined him and confirmed that this was indeed so.

The doctor looked up his records and said: "Ah yes! I see here that your father had exactly the same problem. Maybe this complaint runs in the family."

"Definitely not," replied Billy, emphatically. "Me ol' dad had a bit of a problem, sure enough. But it was quite a different thing. His left leg was a bit longer than his right."

Just Desserts

Old Albert Jones had led a blameless life, but he had fallen on hard times. Then he heard from various disreputable characters in his local down in Hakin that it was possible to survive quite nicely on a spot of occasional shop-lifting at the Spar Supermarket.

So one busy Saturday morning he slipped into the supermarket, looking very furtive, and slipped a tin of pears into the inside pocket of his jacket. Naturally enough, his dastardly deed was picked up on the store's security camera, and he soon found himself in the manager's office being confronted by the local constabulary. And so the cogs of justice began to turn.

In due course Albert was hauled up before the magistrates. Having heard the evidence and having then examined the tin of pears, the Chairman of the Bench said to Albert: "Is this your very first offence?" Albert nodded miserably. "We have to deal with these matters very severely," said the magistrate, "or civilisation will collapse about our ears. Now then, I want that tin of pears opened and the contents counted." The Clerk of the Court found a tin-opener, did the honours, and in due course reported that there were four pears in the can.

"Now just you listen to me," said the Magistrate to Albert. "This is your first offence, so I shall be lenient. I am going to sentence you to four days in prison, one for each pear that you stole. And let that be a lesson to you!"

"Thank you, yer Honour," said Albert, greatly relieved. "And thank God I put back that bloody tin o' baked beans!"

Really Moving

In the good old days when there used to be a fair amount of rail traffic in and around Whitland Railway Station, an American visitor was standing on the main platform waiting for his train. As he stood there a train went through at considerable speed. Turning to an old porter the American said "Say, that train is really moving!"

"Why no, boy," replied the old porter. "A's not hardly movin' at all. A's only shuntin', which is the next best thing to standin' still. But if tha wants to see'n movin', just tha wait till tha sees'n comin' back th'other way!"

Grounds for Divorce

Bertie Reynolds came from Marloes. He was a man of modest intellect, but he was big and strong, and he managed to get himself a job as a labourer on a housing site in Hakin. Every day the gang of workers would sit down in their little shed at lunch-time and eat their sandwiches and drink their tea. On his first day at work Bertie opened up his lunch-box, examined his sandwiches and let out a loud moan. "Oh no!" he wailed. "Not corned beef and mustard! I hate corned beef and mustard in me sandwiches! But I suppose I'd better eat'em, else I'll starve." And so he ate his sandwiches, muttering and moaning in protest.

Next day Bertie opened up his lunch-box and discovered that his sandwiches contained corned beef and mustard again. He cursed and he groaned, and complained bitterly in front of his mates, but at last he ate them since there was nothing else to eat. On the third day the same thing happened, and on the fourth and fifth. At last his mates could stand the moaning and groaning no more, and one of them said: "Now then, Bertie. If tha hates corned beef an' mustard sandwiches so much, why the hell don't tha complain to thy ol' woman an' tell her to put somethin' else in 'em instead?"

"Good Lord!" said Bertie. "Surely tha don't think I has a wife? If I had, an' she'd have give me these bloody sandwiches day in an' day out, that would surely have bin grounds for divorce. Better off single I am, so I makes me sandwiches meself."

Quite Nice Indeed

Not very long ago, a drugs case was being heard at the Pembrokeshire Quarter Sessions. During the presentation of the evidence, samples of the illegal substances -- in the form of small white tablets -- were passed over to the members of the jury for them to examine. Eventually, upon the completion of all the evidence and the closing addresses by the prosecution and defence, the jury went to the retiring room to consider their verdict.

They were closeted away for an inordinately long period of time, and occasionally loud bursts of laughter were heard by the constable at the door. At last a message was passed out by the foreman of the jury and was handed on to a senior Court official. In turn he approached the judge. "Your Honour," he said. "There is a message from the jury. They say they are having a wonderful time considering the intricacies of this case. They also say that they really enjoyed those little white sweets, and ask if you will be kind enough to have some more sent in to them!"

A Simple Mistake

One of the local landed gentry was playing a round of golf on Tenby Golf Course. As was his wont, he had hired a local lad to act as caddy for him. All went well until they reached the twelfth hole, when the squire lost his ball. After a prolonged search, he at last accused the caddy of having stolen it. The lad denied the charge vehemently, and a few minutes later the squire found the ball himself, off the fairway and in the rough. He began to apologise, but the caddy held his hand up and cut him short. "Never mind, sir," said the lad. "Tha thought I was a thief and I thought tha was a gentleman. There's a funny thing, for it looks like we was both mistaken!"

No Job for a Priest

Tom Irish used to work on building sites round about Haverfordwest, and every Friday after picking up his wages he would hit the bottle in town, stagger home and collapse into bed feeling very much the worse for wear. He would wake up at three o'clock in the morning, quite convinced he was about to die, and he would send his wife off to fetch the Roman Catholic priest to administer the last rites. This happened several times, and each time the priest gave Tom a good ticking off and elicited a promise that he would give up drinking spirits.

At last the priest decided that he would never again get out of bed at three o'clock in the morning for Tom Irish, no matter how urgent the request. But the following Saturday morning, at some unearthly hour, there was a knock on the priest's front door, and Tom's wife stood there as usual. "Come quick, Father!" she said. "Tom is feelin' terrible, and he says he is about to die. Please to come and give'n the last rites."

Against his better judgement the priest got dressed and staggered off down the road to Tom's house, only half awake but knowing that if there really was something seriously wrong with Tom he would be failing in his calling if he failed to turn out. When he arrived Tom was in a terrible state. "Oh Father, Father!" he wailed. "This time I knows my time has really come. Look at all them little mice crawlin' all over the ceilin', and look at all them big black rats creepin' up the curtains an' all over the walls, an' there is a big black snake under me bed! They are goin' to eat me up, an' me white bones will rot in hell!"

Upon this the priest put his hand in his pocket, took out his wallet and said; "Tom Irish, there is nothing more I can do for you. It's not a priest you want. Here's ten bob. Now for God's sake go out and get yourself a fox terrier and leave me in peace!"

Just a bit of Favouritism

Mary Murphy and her husband Seamus were good Catholics, and they had been living in Merlin's Bridge for many years. They had fifteen children, who all appeared to live in reasonable harmony. Many of the neighbours wondered how on earth they managed to get by on Seamus's small wages. One day a BBC reporter, who was doing a programme about large families, came to see them. He wanted to press Mary on the frictions and rivalries that must exist when so many small children were living cheek by jowl, and he asked Mary if any of the children were her particular favourites. "Oh yes indeed," replied Mary. "Some of them are my great favourites, and I'll do absolutely anything for them."

"Oh? And which ones might they be?" asked the reporter, holding the microphone out for her reply. "The ones who are miserable, until they cheer up," said Mary. "And the ones who are sick, until they get better. And the ones who are away, until they get home."

Chapter Seven

LOVE AND MARRIAGE

Not Overdoing It

It was coming up to St Valentine's Day, and Harry Hurry (who was well known for his caution in all things) went in to the florists shop in Bridge Street in Haverfordwest. Looking nervously about him, he said: "I wants a few nice flowers to send to a lady, if you please."

The florist sensed that she was in at the beginning of a great romance, and said: "You can do no better than to say it with flowers, sir. May I suggest our £5 bouquet of mixed daffodils and tulips with delicate greenery, or perhaps a couple of dozen red roses? The latter, in particular, will say a great deal."

Harry thought about these suggestions for a long time, and finally said: "No, I reckons that three daffodils will be about right. I don't want to say too much."

A Lovely Likeness

Mrs Bertha Beynon was walking along Charles Street in Milford pushing her pram. An old friend of hers came by, peeped into the pram and said: "Ooh, isn't he lovely! Just like his father."

"I know," said Bertha. "Bloody nuisance. It's a real shame he don't look more like my husband!"

Better Late than Never

Old Aunt Lizzie was ninety-three years old but still sprightly enough to get to church and to confession. But she was slowing down, and this worried her greatly.

One day she turned up at confession and said: "Father, I have sinned. I have committed adultery with a seventeen-year-old gardener behind the greenhouse down at Scotchwells, and I have done wicked deeds with the Chairman of the Council in the middle of the Bridge Meadow."

"Good gracious!" said the priest. "In this last week? And at your age?"

"Why no boy," replied Aunt Lizzie. "This was seventy years ago. I felt a bit miserable this mornin' and felt like recallin' some pleasant experiences."

Keeping it Quiet

Walt Double Malt, a well-known resident of Martletwy, had problems with his wife, especially when he returned home drunk at two o'clock in the morning. Early one Sunday morning, after a night on the tiles, he let himself in through the back door and had an inspired idea. He fetched an old length of clothes-line from the cupboard and laboriously tied to it all the pots, pans, trays and cutlery he could find. He then proceeded upstairs dragging the whole lot behind him and saying to the cat: "I don't know what you thinks, Moggins, but I reckons she'll never hear me comin' upstairs with all this racket goin' on!"

Better than Shoes

Billy Morris of Haverfordwest was feeling in a generous mood, and decided to get his wife a nice pair of shoes for her birthday. So he went into Mr Shearn the cobbler to get something posh made up for her. After discussing size, style and so forth Billy said "She has a bit of trouble with her ankles, poor dab. What would you recommend to put things right?"

"Well," said Mr Shearn. "I don't think you could do better than rubber heels." "Is that so?" replied Billy. "That sounds like pretty good advice. But what shall I rub'em with?"

A Matter of Chance

A good-looking lady in her forties got onto the bus from Johnston to Haverfordwest, with one pair of twins in tow and another younger pair in a big pram. When they were all settled into the bus, the conductor said: "What a blessing for you -- two pairs o. twins. Tell me -- do you always get twins?"

"Oh no!" said the lady, blushing slightly. "Thousands of times we don't get anything at all!"

Female Intuition

Betty worked for John Francis the Estate Agents in Haverfordwest, in the days before it got big by buying up the Halifax. She went in to work one day and found that Mabel, the secretary, was showing off a large new engagement ring and was feeling very pleased with herself.

Betty said: "Oh, what a pretty ring! Let me see now -- I bet the man who gave it to you was tall, with blue eyes and light brown hair, a fine way with words a fast car and a butterfly tattooed on his backside."

Mabel blushed slightly and said "You are quite right! What wonderful female intuition!"

"No such luck," said Betty "That ring is the very one I gave back to him just a fortnight ago."